# The Gold Rush

### Companion Book for *Gold Rush*

20/52
£2
Tr.

Text and Photographs by
## Ian and Sally Wilson
Illustrations by Sally Wilson

Gordon Soules Book Publishers Ltd.
West Vancouver, Canada
Seattle, U.S.A

Available in the Exploring Canada series:
THE ARCTIC
THE PIONEERS
THE GOLD RUSH
THE VOYAGEURS

Text and illustrations © 2001 by Ian and Sally Wilson

PUBLISHED IN CANADA BY GORDON SOULES BOOK PUBLISHERS LTD.
1359 Ambleside Lane, West Vancouver, B.C.  V7T 2Y9
PUBLISHED IN THE U.S.A. BY GORDON SOULES BOOK PUBLISHERS LTD.
PMB 620, 1916 Pike Place #12,  Seattle, WA  98101-1097
(604) 922-6588    fax: (604) 688-5442
email: books@gordonsoules.com    web site: www.gordonsoules.com

**National Library of Canada Cataloguing in Publication Data**

Wilson, Ian, 1955-
  The gold rush

(Exploring Canada series)
ISBN 1-894661-04-4

1. Klondike River Valley (Yukon)--Gold discoveries--Juvenile
literature. 2. Frontier and pioneer life--Northwest, Canadian--
Juvenile literature. 3. Klondike River Valley (Yukon)--Description
and travel--Juvenile literature. I. Wilson, Sally, 1955- II. Title. III.
Series: Exploring Canada series (West Vancouver, B.C.)
FC4022.3.W44 2001        j971.9'102        C2001-910010-8
F1095.K5W54 2001

Printed and bound in Canada

Book design and graphics by Elisa Gutiérrez
Edited by Anne Norman

# Contents

# What is a gold rush?

A gold rush is a race to an area where gold has been discovered. There have been gold rushes all over the world.

In 1897, there was a gold rush to the Klondike area in the Yukon. This one began when a ship came from the Yukon carrying gold worth more than a million dollars. The 68 miners on board were rich!

Newspapers announced: "Gold! Gold in the Klondike!" People believed they would strike it rich if they went to the Klondike. More than 100,000 people started out for the gold-fields. Few knew how to mine for gold or how hard it would be to get to the Klondike.

**Going to the Klondike**

## A TON AND A HALF OF GOLD!

Sixty-eight passengers on a North American steamship recently reached civilization from the far north. The passengers were mostly miners, direct from the Klondike placer mining districts. The men brought back one and one-half tons of gold in nuggets and dust, worth more than $1,000,000.

This news from the Klondike will no doubt tempt scores of hardy and adventurous spirits to seek a fortune in the frozen North!

### JULY 1897

What people might have read in 1897

People were excited about the Klondike gold-fields because the gold was easy to mine. It was called placer gold. This kind of gold can be mined with just a pick, shovel, pan, and other simple tools.

At the time of the gold rush, many people were unemployed. Thousands of people became caught up in the excitement and headed north. They were called stampeders because they were in a hurry to get to the gold-fields. After all, the newspapers suggested there was gold in every creek and under every bush!

# Where is the Klondike?

The Klondike gold-fields are in the Yukon Territory of Canada. People came from around the world to look for gold!

There were no roads to the Klondike at the start of the gold rush. Most stampeders took a boat north along the coast of British Columbia, then hiked over the Chilkoot Pass. Others took horses along the Stikine Trail. Finally, the stampeders floated down the Yukon River to the gold-fields. ✸

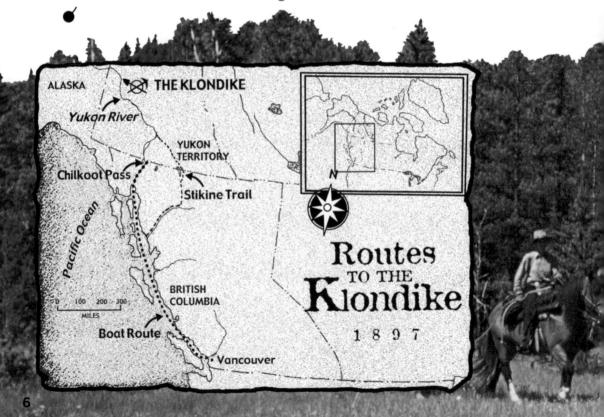

ALASKA

THE KLONDIKE

Yukon River

Chilkoot Pass

YUKON TERRITORY

Stikine Trail

Pacific Ocean

0   100   200   300
MILES

BRITISH COLUMBIA

Boat Route

Vancouver

N

## Routes TO THE Klondike
1897

# Following the stampeders

To learn more about the gold rush, Sally and I decided to follow in the footsteps of the stampeders for one year.

For our trip back in time, we packed the same kind of equipment that stampeders had used. We travelled with horses and climbed over mountains. We even built a boat and floated to the gold-fields.

Come with us on a great adventure as we search for gold in the Klondike!

Ian and Sally on the trail

# Klondike Ho!

A stampeder
going to the
Yukon

"**K**londike Ho!" people shouted when they heard about gold in the Yukon. They packed their supplies and rushed north. Each person hoped to get to the gold-fields before the others. The stampeder in the drawing is ready to go, with a pick and shovel, a gold pan, and other supplies for mining.

# What would you take?

Loading a
packhorse

The first stampeders to arrive in the Klondike did not bring enough food. Many went hungry during the winter of 1897–98. After that, the police made a rule. Everyone coming to the Klondike had to bring enough supplies for one year.

Stampeders were told to take one ton (the weight of a small car) of supplies. What would you take for an entire year? Make a list of what you would need, including food, clothing, and tools for mining.

Stampeders could bring only canned or dried food that would not go bad. They had to get all their supplies to the Klondike on horses, on their backs over steep trails, and in small boats down the Yukon River.

# Travelling with horses

**L**ike many stampeders, Sally and I decided that travelling with horses would be better than carrying our own supplies to the Klondike. First we learned to pack the horses and care for them. Then we began our trip along the Stikine Trail through northern British Columbia.

Outlaw

Dusty

We each had one horse to ride and another to carry our supplies. We sat in our saddles, one hand holding the reins and the other holding a rope tied to the packhorse behind us. Our saddles swayed from side to side as the horses walked tirelessly along the trail.

Each day, the horses carried us through swamps and across deep rivers. At night we

Blackie

Mare

fell asleep to the jingle of their bells as they ate grass near our tent.

As we continued, the trail became muddier and harder to find. Each time our horses became stuck in the mud we thought of the 2000 stampeders who had tried to follow this trail. Most had to turn back and take a different route to the Klondike.

After four weeks, we could no longer find the trail. We had to turn back too. But we were still eager to get to the gold-fields. We decided to take the Chilkoot Pass instead.

**Ian crossing a river**

Ian climbing the
Chilkoot

# Climbing the Chilkoot Pass

**S**ally and I left our horses with friends because the Chilkoot Pass was too steep for horses to climb. Then we travelled by boat along the coast to the start of the trail. Like stampeders, we would have to carry everything on our backs.

With bulging packs, we began the long climb over the mountains. Sally and I crawled over rocks as big as cars. Sweat poured down our faces. It was hard work, but each step took us closer to the Klondike.

It took us one week to climb over the Chilkoot Pass with our supplies. Many stampeders had to make 30 or 40 trips. It took those people three months to carry all their supplies to the other side.

During the gold rush, steps were cut into the steep snow. Gold-seekers trudged up the hill in a long line with heavy loads on their backs. During the winter of 1897–98, more than 10,000 people hiked this trail on their way to the Klondike.

Stampeders climbing the Chilkoot Pass

# Building a boat

**A**fter the stampeders crossed the mountains, their next challenge was to build boats to float down the Yukon River. There were no stores where they could buy boards, so they cut down trees and made their own.

Sawing boards by hand was hard work. One person stood on a platform and struggled to pull the large saw upwards. The other person stood underneath, and

Sally building a boat

was showered with sawdust while pulling the saw down.

Many people built box-shaped boats called scows because they were easier to make than boats with pointed ends. Sally and I decided that a scow was a good choice for us, too.

We nailed long boards together, then pounded cotton into the cracks between the boards. Finally, we sealed each crack with tar so the boat wouldn't leak.

Stampeders building a boat

After two weeks of work, we pulled the scow to the water. Like stampeders long ago, we cheered when it floated. Then we loaded our supplies into the scow and continued our journey to the Klondike. ▷

# By SCOW down the Yukon River

For much of the way down the Yukon River, it was easy travelling. If the wind blew from the right direction, we raised our sail and enjoyed a free ride. The current of the river also carried our scow along at a fast pace with little effort from us.

There were some dangerous rapids though. During the gold rush, many boats flipped over in the waves. Imagine making it all the way north, climbing the Chilkoot Pass, and then losing everything when your boat sank. Fortunately, Sally and I avoided the largest waves and had a safe journey.

Sally and I stopped at many creeks along the way to pan for gold. During the gold rush, stampeders found placer gold all along the Yukon

16

River. Some people made their fortune before even reaching the Klondike.

Sally and I didn't find any gold at the creeks. We continued down the river from dawn to dusk each day, eager to get to the gold-fields.

We finally reached the Klondike after a month on the river. Now we could call ourselves Klondikers. Like gold-seekers long ago, we laughed and cheered. We also hoped that there was some gold left for us.

# Panning for gold

As soon as stampeders arrived in the Klondike, they headed to the gold-fields to pan for gold. They had to hurry though, because everyone was rushing to claim the best ground. In the photograph, Sally is testing her first pan. The look on her face tells me she isn't a millionaire yet!

All methods of separating gold from the dirt involve gravity. Gold is almost 20 times heavier than water and much heavier than any other rocks found with it. Because gold is so heavy, it will always sink to the bottom of a gold pan.

**Sally panning for gold**

Miners have been using gold pans of various shapes and sizes for thousands of years. You can try panning with a pie tin.

1. Fill the pan half full of dirt or gravel from a place where you think there might be gold.

2. Fill the pan with water and break up any lumps of dirt by hand.

3. Put the pan under water and shake the pan from side to side to allow the heavy gold to settle to the bottom.

4. Lift the pan out of the water. Tip it slightly to allow the lighter material at the top to flow out with the water.

5. Repeat steps 3 and 4 several times.

6. Pick out the larger pieces of gravel by hand.

7. Repeat steps 3 and 4 until only the heaviest sand and gold remain in the bottom of the pan.

8. Gently pour out the water and claim your gold!

# Staking a claim

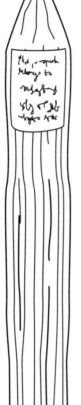

**M**iners can't start digging for gold just anywhere. They must "stake a claim" to be allowed to mine the land they have chosen.

First, they visit the Mining Office to make sure no one else has registered a claim for that land. If the claim is available, the miner drives two wooden stakes into the ground to claim the land.

Even today, anyone over 18 years old can stake a claim in the Klondike. It costs only $10. With dreams of huge nuggets, Sally and I staked our own claim. We panned for more than a week but found only a few small flecks of gold.

Although there was very little gold on that claim, we planned to keep looking in other places until we struck it rich. 🦋

20

# A Klondike home

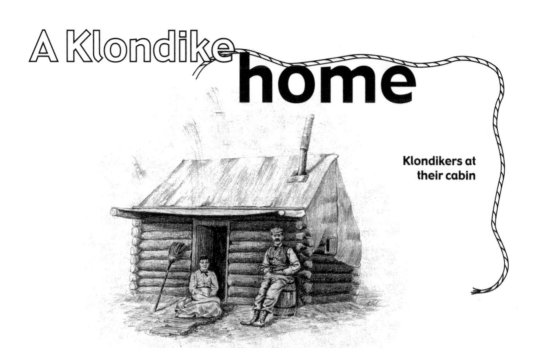

**Klondikers at their cabin**

**B**efore winter came, Klondikers needed a place to stay. Many people built log cabins from trees in the area. Others used the tents they had brought on the trip, or they made shacks with boards taken from their scows.

Klondike homes had no running water and no indoor toilets. Many cabins had only dirt floors and canvas for window panes.

If a man was with his wife, they might try to make their home more cheerful with curtains and other decorations. Most Klondikers didn't mind living in simple cabins because they were sure they would soon be rich.

# Women in the Klondike

Although most of the Klondikers were men, many women also went to the gold-fields. Some came with their husbands to help dig for gold. Other women came on their own, hoping to strike it rich.

Women found it hard to climb the Chilkoot Pass dressed in the ankle-length skirts that were worn back then. Their thin boots gave little support when stepping from boulder to boulder. Still, the women continued despite the hardships.

**Working on a claim**

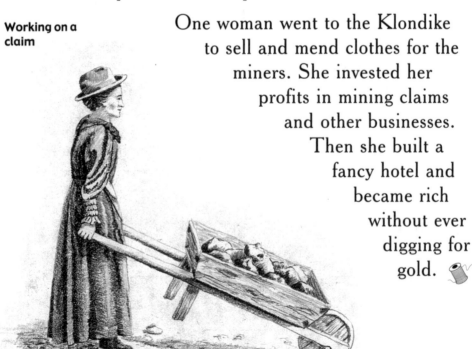

One woman went to the Klondike to sell and mend clothes for the miners. She invested her profits in mining claims and other businesses. Then she built a fancy hotel and became rich without ever digging for gold.

# A northern winter

Sally and I spent our winter at the log cabin shown in this photograph. Like Klondikers long ago, we lived a simple life. We used a woodburning stove for heat and a small lantern for light.

Each morning we took turns carrying buckets of water from the river. We needed two buckets a day for drinking, cooking, and washing. We also took turns chopping wood for the stove. Our life wasn't all work, though. On warmer days we put on our snowshoes and followed animal tracks through the forest.

Klondikers spent their days doing chores and looking for gold. Winter was a lonely time for those who were far from their families and friends. They spent their evenings reading or playing cards by candlelight.

**Life in a cabin**

The days in mid-winter were short and cold. In December the sun rose at 10:30 in the morning and set at 2:30 in the afternoon. The temperature often dropped to -50°C. Friendships were strained in the cramped, tiny cabins. Many people became irritable after being inside for too long.

Luckily, Sally and I got along well through the winter. Even so, we looked forward to the longer days of late winter when we could spend more time outside and look for gold.

**Playing cards**

# Hauling supplies

When miners needed food or supplies, they travelled from the gold-fields to the stores in Dawson City. It often took a day or more to snowshoe there. It took even longer for each miner to return with a toboggan-load of supplies.

To learn what life had been like for miners, Sally and I travelled for several weeks by snowshoe. Like them, we hauled toboggans loaded with our food and clothing. It was hard work. However, it was the only means of winter transportation for Klondikers, unless they had a dog team or horses.

Sally hauling a toboggan

# Mining during winter

**M**iners were so eager to find gold that many worked through the winter. To mine during cold weather, they shovelled away the snow where they thought there might be gold. Then they lit fires to thaw the ground.

The ground thawed a little at a time. Miners used picks and shovels to fill buckets with dirt. Each evening they would pan out the dirt to see if there was gold where they had worked. Some miners became millionaires over the winter. Others found nothing.

Ian steam thawing

One day a miner discovered a better way to thaw the ground. He used a pipe with steam coming out the end.

This method, called steam thawing, was much faster and easier than building fires. The pipe was pushed into the ground and the steam thawed the soil.

On our snowshoe trip, Sally and I met a miner named Jerry Bryde. He was mining during winter just as Klondikers had long ago. We helped Jerry use his steam boiler so he could search for gold.

**Jerry and Sally at the steam boiler**

# Mining for gold

## A rocker box

During the gold rush, miners often used rocker boxes to separate gold from the dirt. As its name suggests, a rocker box has rockers on the bottom. It is tipped from side to side like a baby's cradle.

In this photograph, Sally is shovelling dirt into a tray at the top of the box. Then she poured several scoops of water onto the dirt. The tray had holes in it so the dirt, water, and gold would pass through. Large rocks remained in the tray. Sally tossed them out each time the tray became full.

**Sally using a rocker box**

As with a gold pan, the heavy gold sank directly to the bottom of a rocker box. Along the bottom, a series of ridges called riffles trapped the gold. The water flushed the rest of the dirt and rocks out the bottom end of the rocker box.

The largest pieces of gold, called nuggets, became trapped in the riffles at the upper end of the rocker box. Fine gold and flakes were carried farther down before being trapped near the bottom.

**Working at a rocker box**

Again and again, we shovelled in dirt, poured in water, then rocked the box from side to side. After several hours of work we checked the riffles. A few small nuggets glistened in the sunlight! This was our reward for all the hard work.

Sally working at a sluice box

# A sluice box

If Klondikers had enough water on their claim, they used a sluice box to mine for gold. A sluice box is a long, narrow trough with riffles on the bottom.

The miner shovels dirt into the upper end. As water flows through the sluice, it carries the dirt out the bottom end.

Gold is caught by the riffles on the bottom of the sluice box. In this photograph, Sally is pulling large rocks out of the way at the bottom end of the sluice box. She was careful not to dislodge the gold trapped in the riffles.

# Facts about gold

 Gold is so valuable that one ounce is worth almost $400. Its value changes each day.

Each year, almost $2 billion worth of gold is mined in Canada.

 Gold weighs nearly 20 times as much as water and twice as much as lead.

 Gold is so heavy that you could not pick up a piece the size of a loaf of bread.

 Gold is not much harder than a fingernail. It can be pounded so thin that light can pass through it.

 Gold can't be picked up with a magnet.

 Gold is one of the best conductors of electricity.

 Gold has been mined for more than 7000 years.

# Hydraulic mining

**W**orking with a shovel was a slow way to move large amounts of dirt. Hydraulic mining was much faster. This type of mining uses water flowing through pipes to flush dirt into a sluice box.

In the photograph, Sally is directing the flow of water through a large nozzle to bring dirt down the hill. The water and dirt flow through the sluice. The heavy gold is trapped in riffles along the bottom. Our friend Jerry is clearing large rocks out of the sluice box.

**Hydraulic mining**

# Golden memories

**A good clean-up**

When the riffles in a sluice box or rocker box were full of gold and heavy minerals, miners looked forward to a clean-up. As they cleaned out the riffles, the miners finally collected the gold they had worked so hard for.

With the same excitement miners felt 100 years earlier, Sally and I helped with a clean-up. We scooped spoonfuls of gold from the sluice box until we had almost $600 worth of gold!

Finding gold was a wonderful way to end our year as Klondikers. As we held the glittering nuggets, we thought of the highlights of our adventure. We will always remember our horses, the scow trip, winter in a log cabin, and, most of all, THE GOLD!

# A gold rush glossary

**Clean-up:** The time when a miner removes gold from a sluice box or rocker box.

**Gold-fields:** An area where gold is found.

**Gold pan:** A round pan used to separate gold from the dirt.

**Nugget:** A large piece of gold.

**Pick:** A long-handled tool with a curved iron bar at one end, used for breaking up hard ground.

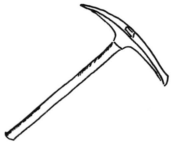

**Placer gold:** Gold that can be easily mined with hand tools.

**Riffles:** Ridges on the bottom of a sluice box or rocker box. The riffles trap gold.

**Rocker box:** A cradle-shaped box that is rocked back and forth to separate gold from the dirt.

**Scow:** A square boat.

**Sluice box:** A long trough with ridges on the bottom, used to separate gold from the dirt.

**Stake a claim:** To mark out a piece of ground or place as your own.

**Stampeders:** People who rushed to the Klondike to look for gold.

**Steam thawing:** Using steam to thaw the frozen ground during winter.

**Strike it rich:** To find gold or other riches.

## About the authors

Ian and Sally Wilson are Canadian best-selling authors and wilderness adventurers. They have written nine books and numerous articles for children's magazines and school textbooks. Their writings are based on their personal experiences exploring Canada's wilderness during the past 20 years and their research of Canada's history. They have also shared their knowledge with radio and TV audiences and with children at more than 1000 schools across Canada.

## Books in the Exploring Canada Series

A series of children's books by Ian and Sally Wilson

**THE VOYAGEURS**
36 pages, ISBN 1-894661-01-X, $7.95

**THE GOLD RUSH**
36 pages, ISBN 1-894661-04-4, $7.95

**THE ARCTIC**
36 pages, ISBN 1-894661-02-8, $7.95

**THE PIONEERS**
36 pages, ISBN 1-894661-03-6, $7.95

## Full-length books by Ian and Sally Wilson

**WILDERNESS JOURNEY:** *Reliving the Adventures of Canada's Voyageurs*
248 pages, ISBN 0-919574-74-2, $16.95   **A full-length book to accompany *The Voyageurs***

**GOLD RUSH:** *Reliving the Klondike Adventure in Canada's North*
248 pages, ISBN 0-919574-59-9, $16.95   **A full-length book to accompany *The Gold Rush***

**ARCTIC ADVENTURES:** *Exploring Canada's North by Canoe and Dog Team*
248 pages, ISBN 0-919574-43-2, $16.95   **A full-length book to accompany *The Arctic***

**WILDERNESS SEASONS:** *Life and Adventure in Canada's North*
208 pages, ISBN 0-919574-34-3, $16.95   **A full-length book to accompany *The Pioneers***

**WILD AND FREE:** Living with Wildlife in Canada's North
192 pages, ISBN 0-919574-87-4, $16.95

**All of Ian and Sally Wilson's books are published by Gordon Soules Book Publishers Ltd.**